Let's Explore
Venus

Helen and David Orme

GARETH**STEVENS**

PUBLISHING

A Member of the WRC Media Family of Companies

Please visit our web site at: **www.garethstevens.com**
For a free color catalog describing Gareth Stevens Publishing's list
of high-quality books and multimedia programs, call
1-800-542-2595 (USA) or 1-800-387-3178 (Canada).
Gareth Stevens Publishing's fax: (414) 332-3567.

Library of Congress Cataloging-in-Publication Data

Orme, Helen-
    Let's explore Venus / Helen and David Orme.
        p. cm. — (Space launch!)
    Includes index.
    ISBN-13: 978-0-8368-7950-6 (lib. bdg.)
    ISBN-13: 978-0-8368-8135-6 (softcover)
    1. Venus (Planet)—Juvenile literature. I. Orme, David, 1948 Mar. 1- II. Title.
    QB621.O76   2006
    523.42—dc22   2006034868

This North American edition first published in 2007 by
Gareth Stevens Publishing
A Member of the WRC Media Family of Companies
330 West Olive Street, Suite 100
Milwaukee, Wisconsin 53212 USA

This U.S. edition copyright © 2007 by Gareth Stevens, Inc. Original edition copyright © 2006 by ticktock Entertainment
Ltd. First published in Great Britain in 2006 by ticktock Media Ltd., Unit 2, Orchard Business Centre, North Farm Road,
Tunbridge Wells, Kent, TN2 3XF, United Kingdom.

The publishers would like to thank: Sandra Voss, Tim Bones, James Powell, Indexing Specialists (UK) Ltd.

Ticktock project editor: Julia Adams
Ticktock project designer: Emma Randall

Gareth Stevens Editorial Direction: Mark Sachner
Gareth Stevens Editors: Barbara Kiely Miller and Carol Ryback
Gareth Stevens Art Direction: Tammy West
Gareth Stevens Designer: Dave Kowalski

Photo credits (t=top, b=bottom, c=center, l=left, r=right, bg=background)

Bridgeman Art Library: 15b; ESA: 21, 22, 23tl; NASA: front cover, 1, 7tr, 7bl, 13tl, 18tl, 18cr, 20tl, 20tl (inset), 20br; Science Photo Library:
4–5bg (original); Shutterstock: 3bg, 7tl, 11tl, 11cr, 13tr, 16bl, 23br; ticktock picture archive: 5tr, 6, 6–7bg, 8bl, 8cr, 9, 9–10bg, 10, 11b, 12c, 13bl,
14, 14–15bg, 15tl, 16tr, 16br, 17tr, 17bl, 18–19bg, 19tr, 19bl, 20br (inset), 22–23bg. Rocket drawing Dave Kowalski/© Gareth Stevens, Inc.

Every effort has been made to trace the copyright holders for the photos used in this book. The publisher apologizes,
in advance, for any unintentional omissions and would be pleased to insert the appropriate acknowledgements in
any subsequent edition of this publication.

Printed in Canada

1 2 3 4 5 6 7 8 9 10 10 09 08 07 06

Contents

Words in the glossary are printed in **bold** the first time they appear in the text.

Where Is Venus?

There are eight known planets in our **solar system**. The planets travel around the Sun. Venus is the second closest planet to the Sun.

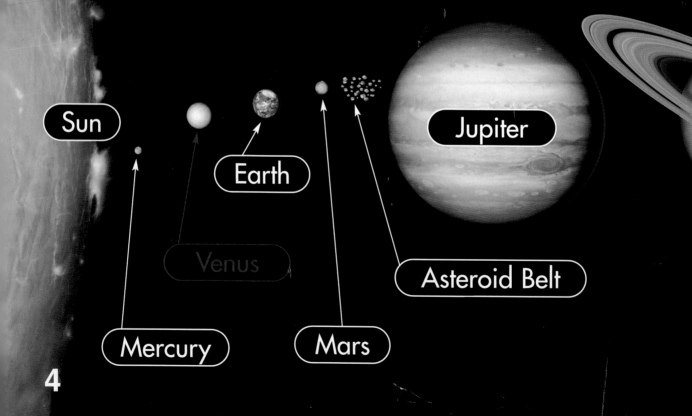

Sun

Earth

Jupiter

Venus

Asteroid Belt

Mercury

Mars

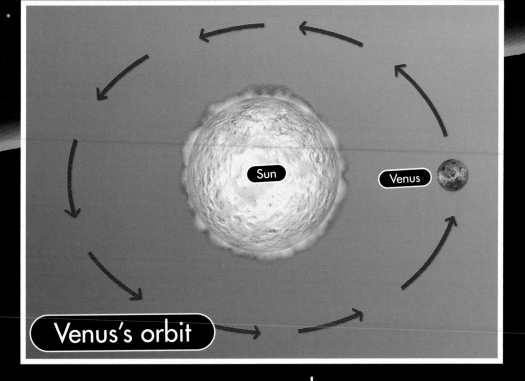

The time a planet takes to travel around the Sun once is called a year. Venus travels around the Sun once every 225 **Earth days**. This journey is called Venus's **orbit**.

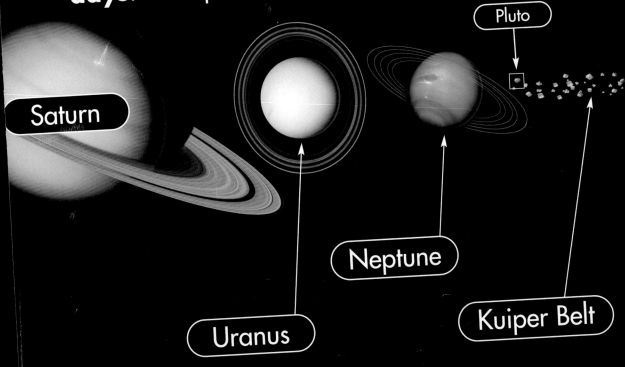

Venus is a very hot planet. It is covered by thick clouds. We cannot see through the clouds with a telescope. But **space probes** can use special telescopes to take pictures of the planet.

This is a drawing of Venus's surface. It is mostly flat and very dry. There is no water on Venus.

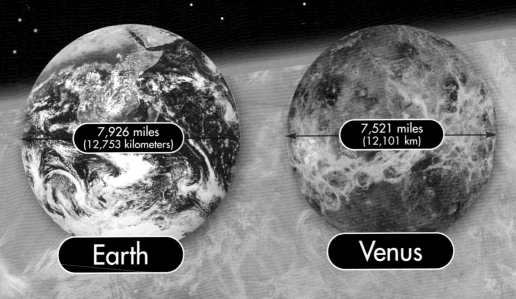

Earth

7,926 miles
(12,753 kilometers)

Venus

7,521 miles
(12,101 km)

Venus is almost the same size as Earth.
It is sometimes called Earth's twin.

direction of spin

Planets are always spinning.
The time a planet takes
to spin around once
is called a day.
One day on Venus
is the same length
of time as 243
Earth days!

Venus spins in the
opposite direction
of Earth.

Venus is the hottest of all the planets. It is even hotter than Mercury, even though that planet is closer to the Sun.

The top temperature on Venus is about 896 °Fahrenheit (480 °Celsius)!

The highest temperature on Mercury is about 806 °F (430 °C)

The highest temperature measured on Earth is 136 °F (58°C).

On Earth, water freezes at a temperature of 32 °F (0 °C).

900 °F

800 °F

700 °F

600 °F

500 °F

400 °F

300 °F

200 °F

100 °F

0 °F

−100 °F

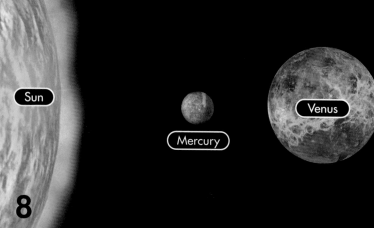

Sun

Mercury

Venus

The **atmosphere** on Venus is very thick and heavy. It pushes down toward the surface of the planet. The pressure on Venus would crush a person right away!

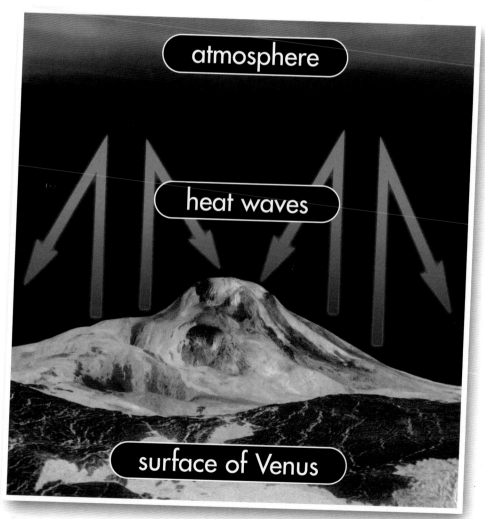

atmosphere

heat waves

surface of Venus

This picture shows how the thick and heavy atmosphere stops heat from escaping from Venus's surface. The trapped heat is what makes Venus so hot.

Global Warming

The atmosphere on Venus is mostly made of a gas called **carbon dioxide.** This gas stops nearly all of the heat on Venus from escaping into space. People worry that Earth may become like Venus.

The heat from the Sun reaches Venus's surface.

Sun

The thick atmosphere traps the heat, so the planet can never cool down.

Venus

atmosphere

On Earth, we make a lot of carbon dioxide. We make it when we burn oil or coal. Cars, factories, and planes all make this gas.

The gas becomes trapped in Earth's atmosphere. It stops heat from escaping from Earth. We call this **global warming**.

Could Earth end as up hot and dry as Venus?

Earth today

Earth in the future?

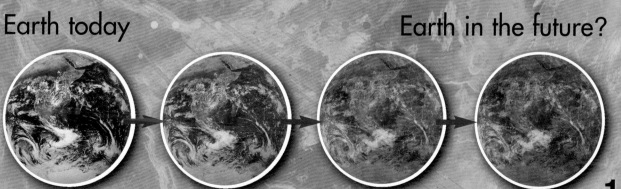

On the Surface

Space probes use machines to discover what is hidden under Venus's clouds. The probes can tell scientists a lot about the planet's surface.

Scientists have used the information collected by space probes to make special maps of the planet.

This is a picture of Venus that scientists have made. They use different colors for the different kinds of areas on the planet.

Brown shows very high mountains.

Yellow shows very low valleys.

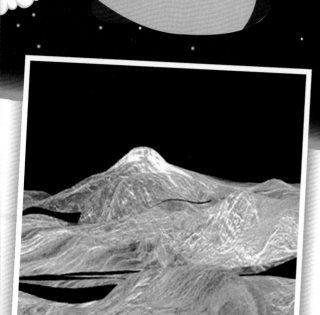

The highest mountain on Venus is called Maxwell Montes. It is about 7 miles (11 km) high.

The highest mountain on Earth is Mount Everest in the Himalayas. It is about 5 ½ miles (9 km) high.

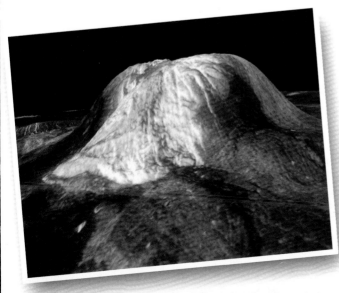

Venus may have **active volcanoes**. A volcano is a mountain where the hot liquid and gases inside the planet burst out of its surface.

Finding Venus

Venus is the brightest of all the planets. It is brighter than any star in the sky. People have always wondered about Venus.

Venus was named after an ancient Roman goddess. Venus was the goddess of love and beauty.

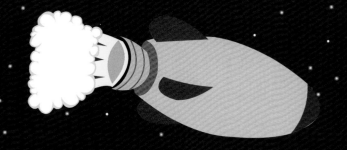

The planet was named Venus because it was a beautiful sight shining in the morning and evening sky.

Thousands of years ago, people could see Venus even though they did not have telescopes or binoculars. In this picture, people are using instruments to find the planets.

What Can We See?

Venus is the easiest planet to see from Earth because it is so bright. You can often see Venus when the sky is still quite light.

Even with a telescope we cannot see details of the planet's surface, because of the thick clouds.

Look for Venus in the early morning . . .

. . . or in the evening.

When Venus passes in front of the Sun, the planet looks like a black dot to us.

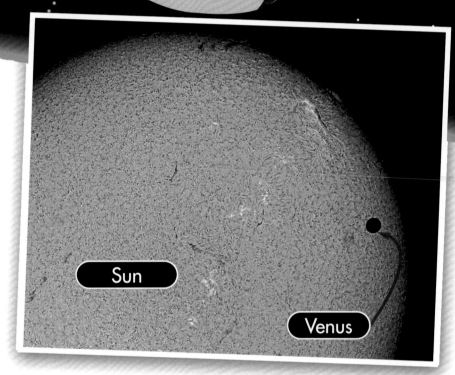

Sun

Venus

This telescope was used to take the picture of Venus in front of the Sun. It is a very special telescope because it protects the scientists' eyes from the Sun.

40 inches (1 meter)

Warning
NEVER look directly at the Sun. It can blind you!

Venus Discoveries

Telescopes cannot see through Venus's thick clouds. Scientists have had to find other ways to study the planet.

Scientists use space probes, like this one, to find out more about far-away planets. This is a photo of the *Pioneer* **orbiter**. It was sent to Venus in 1978.

This painting shows the *Pioneer* orbiter above Venus. It was controlled from Earth, and it had 17 machines to study Venus's temperature and surface.

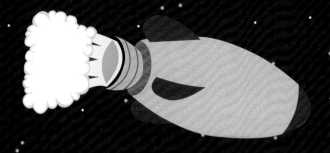

Space probes use **radar**. This tool sends out special radio waves that bounce off parts of objects, such as planets. Radar can help make a 3-D map of all the mountains and valleys on Venus, like this one.

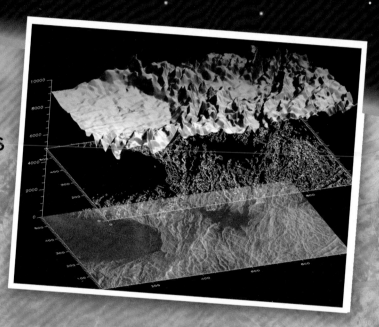

This special 3-D map was also made using radar. It shows many of Venus's mountains and valleys.

Missions to Venus

There have been many space missions to Venus. Some space probes have even landed on the planet. The early Venus space probes were crushed by the atmosphere.

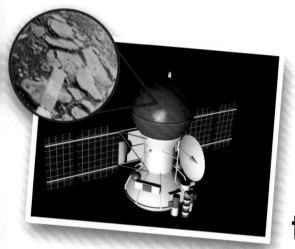

This is the *Venera 9* **lander**. This Russian spacecraft reached Venus in 1975. It was the first lander to take pictures from the surface of the planet. After sending the pictures to Earth for fifty minutes, it was destroyed by the heat on Venus!

In 1989, the United States launched the *Magellan* mission. *Magellan* orbited Venus to make a map of it.

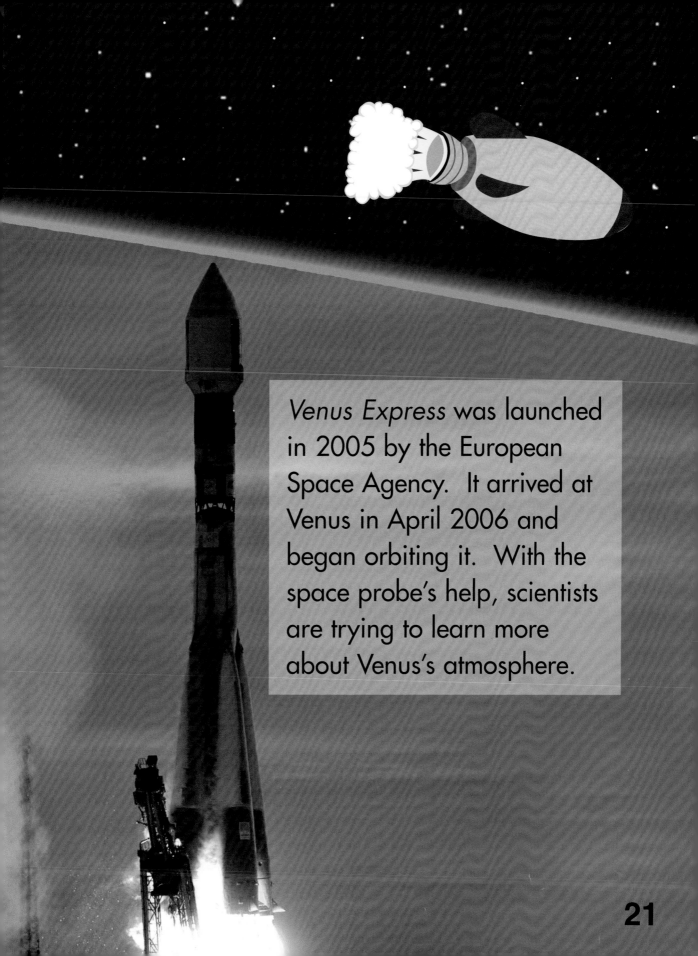

Venus Express was launched in 2005 by the European Space Agency. It arrived at Venus in April 2006 and began orbiting it. With the space probe's help, scientists are trying to learn more about Venus's atmosphere.

new Missions

Venus is too dangerous for people to visit because of its high temperatures and crushing atmosphere. If we want to explore Venus's surface in the future, robots will have to do it for us.

The robots will be controlled by scientists on Earth.

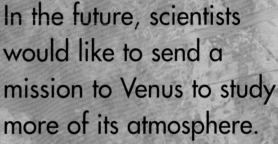

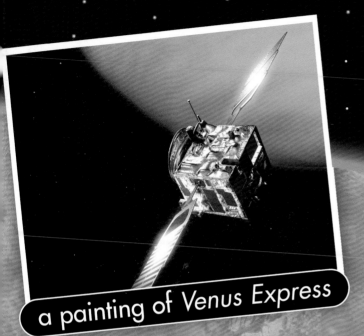

a painting of Venus Express

In the future, scientists would like to send a mission to Venus to study more of its atmosphere.

Usually, scientists look for **microbes**. Some kinds of these tiny forms of life are found in Earth's atmosphere.

If microbes like the ones in Earth's atmosphere are found in the atmosphere of another planet, life might be possible there!

Glossary

active volcanoes volcanoes that are still erupting, giving off gases and melted rock

asteroid a rocky object that orbits the Sun. Most asteroids orbit the Sun between Mars and Jupiter.

atmosphere the gases that surround a planet, moon, or star

carbon dioxide a gas that is made when some things burn

Earth day a day is the time it takes a planet to spin around once. A day on Earth is 24 hours long.

global warming the increase in the temperatures of Earth's atmosphere and oceans. Gases in the atmosphere keep heat from escaping.

lander a spacecraft designed to land on a planet or moon

microbes very tiny living things such as a virus or bacteria

orbit the path that a planet or other object takes when traveling around the Sun, or the path a satellite takes around a planet or moon

orbiter a spacecraft designed to go into orbit around a planet.

radar a machine that locates far-away objects and measures their speed or surfaces. It sends out sound waves that bounce off an object and back to the radar. Waves bounce back faster from objects or surfaces that are closer.

solar system the Sun and everything that is in orbit around it

space probe a spacecraft sent from Earth to explore the solar system

Index